Compass Po

C000183290

Plants, Potions and Oils for Horses

Chris Dyer

C☉MPASS
EQUESTRIAN

Henley-in-Arden

Line illustrations by Carole Vincer
Edited by Toni Webber
Editorial Assistant Clare Harris
Design by Alan Hamp

British Library Cataloguing in Publication Data
A catalogue record for this book is available from
the British Library

ISBN 1-900667-24-X

Published in Great Britain in 1999 by
Compass Equestrian Limited
Cadborough Farm, Oldberrow
Henley-in-Arden, Warwickshire
B95 5NX.

Printed in Great Britain
by Ebenezer Baylis
Worcester

Contents

Geranium ↟ Ginger ↟ Jasmine ↟ Juniper ↟ Lavender ↟ Lemon Lime ↟ Mandarin ↟ Marigold ↟ Orange ↟ Peppermint ↟ Pine Tea tree oil ↟ Violet ↟ White thyme ↟ Ylang ylang

List of Illustrations

Introduction

We live in an age of medical miracles. Multi-million pound pharmaceutical companies turn out pills and potions with unpronounceable, unspellable names and we expect them to cure not only our own ailments but our horses' as well. We may wince as we write a cheque to our vet but we are confident that the problems will be solved.

Yet all around us – in our gardens, in our homes, on our shelves, in hedgerows and fields – are remedies which served our ancestors well. These are the natural remedies. Many of them cost no more than the effort of gathering and preparation. All of them can help to promote and maintain the health of the horse.

They are not a substitute for veterinary care in the case of serious illness or accident. You still need the vet's scientific skills of diagnosis, treatment and prognosis, particularly in prevention and prophylaxis and in containing the spread of infection. But there are many disorders which do not need professional attention and some which seem to respond better to age-old methods than to anything else.

This book outlines a wide variety of natural remedies which the author has used and found effective time and time again. They range from herbal treatments, which come as no surprise, to the unexpected properties of such bizarre items as cobwebs and chimney soot. Finally, there is a section on aromatherapy, where the oils of certain plants (*essential oils*) are mixed with a *base oil* and applied, using massage. These oils may be bought at specialist shops, stored and mixed together for use whenever the need arises.

Author's Note

The use of herbs and 'country cures' has been passed down through the generations. Before the advent of modern veterinary science, herbs and 'potions' were the only available treatments. The near demise of the art of 'Herbology', has been largely due to today's veterinary advances. Yet nature found its own way to make a come back.

Resistance to modern drugs is becoming more and more prevalent, and whilst there are, and always will be, sceptics, what are now called alternative medicines have had to be taken seriously. Ironic really as my grandfather looked on modern medicines with the same scepticism, and thought of them as the alternatives!

More and more people are becoming interested in the use of herbs and other natural products as alternative remedies. I hope this book will give you the basic knowledge to make use of the most common and widely available herbs. You will find that herbs (a term I will use generally for all natural plant remedies) are not only good for the alleviation of injuries and illness but are also invaluable for the health, fitness and well-being of your horse.

As for 'country cures' (by which I mean those which are not herbs but are easily obtainable items such as bicarbonate of soda or cider vinegar, which have been used over the generations), you will find them not only to be effective but also much cheaper than modern remedies. A substantial part of this book will also cover the basics of equine aromatherapy, something I have developed and found most successful in the treatment of everyday strains and injuries.

I have based all my doses on a 15 hh horse unless otherwise stated. To dose a horse or pony of a different size simply divide the dose level by 15 then times by the size of your own horse. For handfuls and such measurements just lessen or add a little.

IMPORTANT POINTS TO REMEMBER
- This book is an aid and not a substitute for modern veterinary techniques.
- You must be careful to pick plants or to obtain them from a supplier who does not use sprays. Herbs must be organic to be of worthwhile use. To use a natural remedy contaminated by sprays or chemicals would completely defeat the object of the exercise.
- None of the herbs in this book can be 'overdosed' so never be afraid to increase the dosage slightly if the injury or illness is not being reduced sufficiently, but do follow the full course suggested first.
- The country cures, unless otherwise stated, must be followed to the letter.

Acknowledgments

Thanks to all the people who through the years have shared their knowledge or helped me in one way or another: Mr Leslie Phillips, Mr Peter Meaden, Anne Holland, Mary Gardiner, Jenni and K.

My love and respect to you all.

Plant Power

AMARANTH

(Love lies bleeding)

I really like the name of this one! You never know I might even get some of you feeling sympathetic towards me… ! However tragic the name this herb is really useful. It can help to stem bleeding and can be used to alleviate diarrhoea and to treat sore mouths.

Amaranth is grown in the garden, it is a herb which grows as high as five feet tall with a blood coloured flower spike. It can even be used as a vegetable if you run out of greens !

For bleeding simply apply a clean leaf to the affected area. An infusion can be used as a mouthwash or to treat digestive disorders. To make the infusion place three or four leaves into boiling water, leave to cool, squeeze the leaves out and remove from the liquid. Administer the cooled liquid to the horse, this should amount to around half a pint.

BASIL

Definitely not named after the infamous TV hotel owner, basil is tranquillity itself. It is mid green in colour and has a fairly wide soft leaf.

Use as a tranquilliser for hard to handle horses, bad travellers and to relieve stress in colicky horses. Mix half a dozen sprigs (jolly little word, sounds like Christmas!) in with the feed, and the horse should become noticeably calmer. I find this good if breaking a particularly awkward youngster, or treating a difficult horse that requires physical treatment. It is also useful for relieving stress during bouts of colic.

For bad travellers, add four sprigs to the morning feed and you will find the horse travels much better. A word of warning: competition horses that travel badly should not be given basil. You will receive no thanks if the horse falls asleep half way through the race or event, so please refer to sage, or to the Aromatherapy section.

Do not feed basil to pregnant mares as it can trigger oestrus which causes the mare to abort.

BASKET WILLOW

Basket willow is found around ponds, streams, and rivers. It normally grows in clumps, with many whips shooting from the bottom of the tree.

Basket willow is a very potent pain killer, but does not have the disadvantages sometimes associated with drugs such as 'Bute'. It is also very good for lowering heart rate, and for 'bleeders'. You will not find any temperamental change in your horse at all; horses love basket willow, and you will not have any problems administering this plant.

Start with two twelve-inch sticks given daily for two days, to a maximum of six sticks per day. By the end of this period you should notice the horse becoming more comfortable. If the reaction is negligible, increase the dose by one twelve inch stick per day until the horse shows signs of relief. The stick should include the leaves in summer. In winter, increase the dose by 50 percent to allow for the lack of leaf growth. Buds have been classified as leaves for the purposes of dosage levels.

Basil   *Basket willow*

Remember that you cannot overdose. I personally have had a horse demolish the top of a whole tree with no ill effect.

For bleeders and horses with high heart rates feed one 12 inch stick per day. Please note that basket willow contains salicylic acid which if used frequently can show up on a drug test (refer to Jockey Club rules, prohibitive substances).

CHIVES

Chives grow in clumps and make a nice border plant for those with gardens. They have tubular like leaves which are dark green in colour and which have a distinctive smell of onions when crushed between your fingers. They are easily identified during the flowering season by a purple bobble which forms on the top of the plant. Chives will (as will marigolds) help to reduce the number of flies in the vicinity. Chives are also very good as a conditioner, and for putting a healthy shine to a horse's coat.

Just grab a handful of stems, chop them up and add them to your horse's feed. Horses do not usually like the taste, so I mix chopped

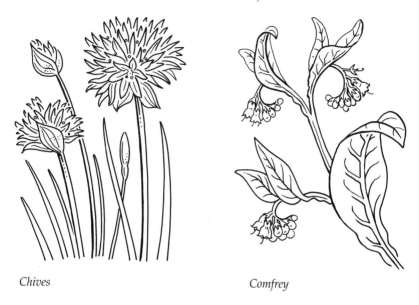

Chives   *Comfrey*

chives with barley meal. You can do this literally as and when you remember, or every day depending on your horse. If you try to remember to add a handful every other day, you cannot go wrong.

You can really experiment with chives as they cannot harm your horse in the slightest.

The other way in which you can use chives is to take a handful of stems, and rub them hard along the neck, shoulders, face, and back of your horse. This will aid in keeping the flies off and help to prevent sweet itch.

COMFREY OR KNITBONE

Comfrey is a large leafed green plant, with a spongy leaf covered with short hairs. It is similar in shape to a dock leaf, but is a much deeper green. The root is white on the inside with a dark brown rind.

There are several types, though the most common is the purple-flowered variety, which is found in most country lane hedgerows, woodlands (mainly indigenous woods) and meadowland. There are two other types of comfrey – the pink-flowered and the white-flowered.

I can offer no explanation for why I have found pink comfrey to be stronger than purple, and white flowered comfrey to be the strongest of all. Comfrey growing in meadowland is my preference as it seems to be slightly stronger.

Comfrey is an extremely versatile herb and can be used in several ways. Purple and pink comfrey will not 'heat' your horse up, although white will if the horse is of a highly strung disposition. You can use the whole of the plant, and even the most finicky eater can be tempted. Horses relish the taste and the only problem is keeping your fingers when feeding it! For those that have a horse that proves me wrong and doesn't like the taste, bash the leaves on a wall or door – then feed, bruising in this case helps.

As you will realise from its common name (Knitbone), this is a powerful herb when used to treat bone damage such as sore shins, chipped knees and arthritis. I have also found it most useful for tendon strains.

Tendon strains

Feed six 10-12 inch leaves per day for 10 days. If the problem is still acute, feed for a further 5 days, adding two 12 inch sticks of basket willow (see basket willow).

Sore shins

Sore shins should be treated by poulticing and through feeding. To poultice, simply soak three leaves of purple comfrey in hot water for around 30 seconds and apply to the horse's shin, bandaging them on in the same way in which you would apply an animalintex. Leave the poultice in place for around two hours and remove. Repeat this for four days and you should start to see a marked improvement.

Rheumatism and arthritis

On the assumption that the horse in question is not in its formative years, pink comfrey is the type you should use. Feed three large leaves per day and, in severe cases, twice a day. It is also advisable to feed basket willow to alleviate the discomfort caused by this condition (see basket willow). If you find your horse is reluctant to take the comfrey, boil approximately five leaves in a covered saucepan, strain the liquid and add to the horses water, about one pint to two gallons. This must be done daily as your horse will not benefit if the 'tea' is not freshly made. I would also advise that you use a cod liver oil supplement or similar.

Chipped knees
Chipped knees and similar injuries should be treated with pink or white comfrey. Comfrey will assist in the repair but it must be understood that the effect of this treatment can only be judged by eye. When your horse has free movement, you may stop the treatment, but until that time you must be meticulous in following the treatment programme.

Up to twenty leaves can be fed depending on the severity of the case. If no improvement is seen within seven days aid the dosage with an extra two pints of comfrey tea to two gallons of water daily.

Stress fractures
Having recently treated a horse with a pelvic stress fracture, I can vouch for the miraculous recovery of an animal that some people thought should be put down. He has benefited to such an extent that after three months he will be going back into training for racing. For injuries as serious as this, white comfrey is the best. Do not be afraid to give plenty. I advise at least forty leaves, and at least one cleaned root per day. The root should ideally be a fresh white colour inside and about half the size of a man's fist. If you cut the rind into slices and add to your horse's normal diet the comfrey will be taken without problems. If for any reason the horse does not relish the root, try grating it and mixing it with rolled barley, or barley meal.

Comfrey can be combined with all other herbs to suit an individual's symptoms. You will accrue enough knowledge as you read on to formulate treatments that will meet your horse's requirements. I would also advise you to look towards your horse's diet to assist in preventing some of the aforementioned problems.

Using Super Solvitax cod liver oil will certainly help as will using a feed that increases calcium intake such as Alfalfa. You will find the two compliment each other in helping to prevent stress related injuries.

COW PARSLEY

Cow parsley is an easy one to remember - it's one your horse nearly wrenches your arms out of their sockets when it tries to snatch a mouthful from the hedgerows. Cow parsley is everywhere - hedges, fields, woods and meadows - and long may it continue! It is a tall plant with a rounded stem similar to celery but joined up. The plant itself is a mid green colour with a large round flower head that has a mass of tiny white flowers. As an extra clue the plant becomes woody and brittle as it dies in the late Autumn. When the plant is dead it is no good.

Cow parsley is a versatile plant, with properties similar to fennel. You can feed as much as you like. The only drawback is that it is available only in spring and summer and unlike many plants does not dry at all well.

Cow parsley aids digestion, has calmative properties and speeds the healing process.

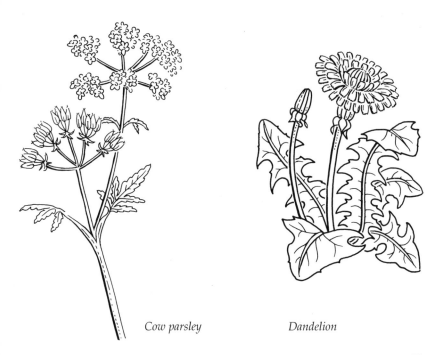

Cow parsley   Dandelion

DANDELIONS

Yes I know you know what they look like but my publisher says I've got to! Dandelions are mid-green with long leaves which have 'teeth' on the edges. Well they look like teeth - hence dandelion. The flowers are bright yellow with small petals and are about an inch across.

Dandelions are good for your horse's overall health. Watch out, I'm going to get technical! They are a great source of beta carotene, potassium and calcium, and have an amazing amount of iron. They are a brilliant diuretic and blood balancer, and are good for the coat.

Dandelions are particularly efficient at relieving the problems of oedema. What clever little chaps they are !

It should be noted that the addition of dandelions to your horse's diet should not have any contradictory effect on any treatment prescribed by your vet.

At each feed, give two dandelion plants, which can include the root if you wish, though the plant will be sufficient. Remember to clean the root if you decide to feed this as well. At this stage, a salt lick should not be present but after three days it should be re-introduced. I would also advise the use of Alfalfa, or Alfa Beet, along with one of the Super Solvitax additives. I mention particular brands because these are my personal preference. There is no substitute for quality, and both these brands have in my experience given value for money. If the oedema is not reducing, remove the salt lick and continue the treatment for a further three days. After this time, reduce the dandelion to one plant per day, until the problem has cleared up.

As a general additive, feed one dandelion every other day, which should be sufficient to keep your horse in good condition. Make sure there is a salt lick available and a constant supply of fresh water because as I have said before dandelions are a diuretic.

DEAD NETTLES

Dead nettles are similar in looks to the common nettle, but have a white or red/purple flower and no sting (honestly). The use of dead nettles is relatively new to me, as I have only recently tried this on my stallion when he damaged his leg. Combined with tea tree, lemon, peppermint and lime oil, the results for me were miraculous.

As the horse was away at another yard, I didn't get to see him for several weeks. He was in great discomfort. As soon as the swelling burst, a large wound opened which wept copiously. I moved him home and started my own treatments. I should say at this point that the vets and also the yard where he had been were concerned over the proud flesh on his leg. It would have to be burned off, they said and copper sulphate and the like were spoken of in hallowed tones.

My first task was to reduce the pain. In an attempt to make the horse more comfortable I fed plenty of basket willow. The basket willow definitely started to work but the horse still exhibited considerable discomfort. As a result of his re-distributing his weight, a very bad abscess developed in the sole on his good foot.

I must admit I was starting to despair. Every day he seemed no better and, being lame on both hind legs, he was losing condition very quickly. I had started to get the original leg under control, but now it flared up again. As the horse transferred the weight from the abscessed foot to the swollen leg, I had a major headache. My girlfriend even suggested I should consider putting him down. I was outwardly horrified, although deep down I had to admit I didn't think she was far from the mark. I included watercress and watermint in his diet and increased his daily dose of cod liver oil by 50 percent. There was a small improvement.

Having opened the abscessed foot, I used a poultice boot lined with comfrey to draw the poison. The horse started to put a little weight back on that leg, but now a third problem arose. The pain he was suffering from two legs had caused him to put his back out. It seemed that I was taking one step forward and two back. I manipulated and corrected the back.

The pain he was in, however still caused me more concern than anything: the basket willow was working, but not sufficiently and he needed something else. That's when I tried the dead nettles. I can't really say why I did so except that I had noticed the horse reaching for some which were just outside his yard and out of reach. Within an hour you could see the difference, he became relaxed and obviously more

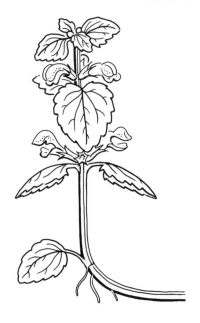 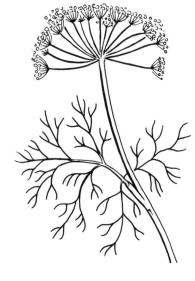

Left Dead nettle   Above Dill

comfortable and he started to whicker at the mares.

I introduced a small amount of eucalyptus into the mix of oils for massage which started to clear the infection in the leg, stopped the proud flesh problem and prevented scarring.

I continued the dead nettles at just three stems a day for three days, along with the basket willow. The horse became more comfortable each day. After the three days I reduced the dead nettles by half, with no sign of the horse's pain returning. I believe the short respite he was given through the combination of these treatments saved the day.

Since then he has been taken off all my treatments and is making a steady recovery. I have now changed his diet, using Alfa Beet as the base to his ration. He receives the identical amount in weight as he did before (he was on sugar beet, rolled barley, and coarse mix). The surprising thing is, his condition is showing a marked improvement on his new diet and he has made better weight gains since his diet change and the increase in cod liver oil. This is not a fluke, as I have put a mare fresh out of training on the same diet, and she is gaining condition daily at a much faster rate than on her previous diet. I am an Alfa Beet, and cod liver oil convert.

The horse received one injection of penicillin when the vet first visited him, and I gave him a shot of long-acting procaine penicillin at the end of my treatment. He will soon be well enough to be turned out for an hour.

I suggest that you use dead nettles in cases of extreme pain and stress and keep to a maximum of three stems (including the flower).

I have since discovered that dead nettles seem to relax bad travellers, without affecting performance. This is something I am researching further.

DILL

Who remembers gripe water? Well that's dill. Dill has a feathery type frond and is bright green in colour.

It is very good at relieving the symptoms of colic, although it won't cure it. Give three or four sprigs of dill to the horse, either crushed or mixed with butter or margarine (See butter). If you crush the dill do it by crushing it in your hands, then place the dill in the horse's mouth, and hold it closed until swallowed. Dill need only be fed when the horse is showing signs of being colicky.

FENNEL

Wonderful stuff! Fennel can be grown virtually anywhere. Try throwing a few seeds on the muck heap, or in that spare space down the side of the stable. If you grow some, try a bit to flavour your next piece of fish.

Fennel has mid to dark green stems with feathery leaves and a distinct aniseed smell and flavour. It comes in two types, Florence and Garden, both of which are fine to use. It can be fed cooked or raw and is eaten with relish.

Fennel has many uses: it is excellent for aiding milk production in lactating mares; for treating blood disorders, and it is good for digestion.

For horses susceptible to colic, fennel should be given on a regular

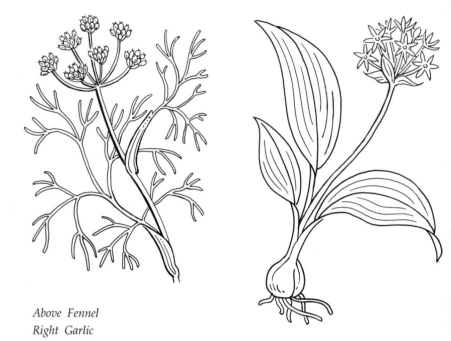

Above Fennel
Right Garlic

basis, as it will help digestion, thereby removing the risk of colic.

For stallions, fennel like cow parsley, will keep a stallion performing vigorously and aid fertility (see cow parsley). Feeding poses no problem as a horse will only take as much as it requires.

GARLIC

Garlic grows wild as well as cultivated. It is normally found close to woodland.

Garlic ! The smell is awful to some people! But it is fantastic stuff. Not only does garlic have the well known effect of keeping stable lads away from stable lasses, but it has almost magical medicinal properties. It is good for the blood, it is anti-bacterial and anti-viral. It relieves the symptoms of Sweet Itch, keeps flies away, and has saved many a young virgin's neck from being bitten! Garlic will also reduce blood pressure in excitable horses and those in competition.

Garlic can be given as a powder purchased from most good food and equestrian shops, but I think feeding the actual clove or an oil based supplement is best.

As a general additive two cloves of garlic should be put in the horse's feed daily. The feeding rates given are for a horse of about 15 hh; you can reduce or increase the dose slightly for a smaller or larger horse.

Horses with Sweet Itch should be given slightly more. I have used garlic on grey horses in an effort to reduce warts and it seems to work.

For horses suffering with a viral infection, garlic is a must. You should feed four cloves per day until the problem has cleared up. Then return to the normal feeding programme of two cloves per day.

In my opinion I do not think that garlic is particularly good for race-horses that are bleeders. I suggest that you look to the other remedies in this book.

HAZEL

Hazel is found in most roadside hedges. It has bright, shiny, mid-brown bark and rounded leaves with serrated edges. It also produces very tasty nuts.

I use hazel when a horse has an infection and it is so simple to

Hazel

administer. Just find a good clean hazel hedge, cut the top shoots from the branches, including the leaves, and feed to your horse. The more you cut the happier your horse will be. So don't be afraid to give him or her a nice big bundle. Hazel also helps condition the coat. In fact, during the summer I give my horses at least an armful a week.

MARIGOLDS

Marigolds are very similar to yellow tansy, the only differences being the colour of the flower, and their potency - marigolds are not as strong as yellow tansy. Marigolds are delightful little orange flowers that are often planted in gardens. If you are unsure of what they look like pop along to your local garden centre and peek at a packet of seeds.

Marigolds make a good fly repellent. I have also found that they can improve coat condition.

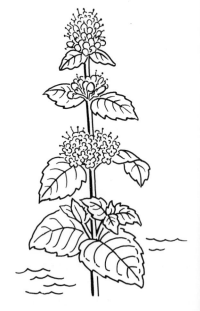

Above Marigold
Right Mentha

Flies hate marigolds particularly if you rub them onto the horse or crush them to make a liquid which can then be poured over the horse. When used in conjunction with cod liver oil and garlic, your horse should have no fly problems. To use as a coat conditioner feed one or two marigolds (flower head and stem) once a week.

MENTHA AQUATICA

Mentha more commonly known as water mint, is found at the edge of most streams and rivers. It is a long slim stemmed plant with ovate leaves, varying from mid green to purple. The plant has a lance like flower head of blue flowers and spindly bright white roots.

Mentha's properties mean that mentha is very good in aiding the treatment of respiratory problems. It is not only of great assistance in the treatment of minor ailments such as coughs, colds and runny noses, but is very good when used to assist horses convalescing from more serious problems such as pneumonia.

There are no hard and fast rules when dosing with mentha but it is wise to give as much as the horse will take (up to three whole plants per day). It is also possible to crush mentha into your horse's water bucket. If you decide to take this course, it is imperative that the water is changed twice daily. Under no circumstances must the water be left as there is the possibility of fermentation, and you may end up with your own version of creme de menthe!

I always find it strange that, with most horses relishing the taste of mint in sweet form, mentha is one of the hardest herbs to administer, I have yet to find a horse that will take the herb readily. In fact some horses are very hard to tempt, and I have found the simplest way to ensure the horse is receiving the benefit is to chop the mentha into small pieces and mix in with the horses food. I have even resorted to 'rolling' the mentha in barley meal.

For everyday colds and coughs continue treatment for five days. In more serious cases for example pneumonia – continue treatment until the problem has cleared completely.

Mentha can also be used as an expectorant by crushing one plant into a bucket and pouring on boiling water. Place the bucket out of reach of your horse and leave in a sealed stable for approximately an hour. This will help to purge your horse's respiratory system. It is advisable for added potency, to use the oils suggested in the aromatherapy section in the mixture. Mentha is also of use in 'bleeders' but must be used with basket willow and nettles to obtain the best results. Mentha will not react against any drug your veterinary surgeon has prescribed.

NASTURTIUMS

Nasturtiums are common to most gardens and can be identified easily, they have large leaves and bright orange flowers. They grow in almost any soil and 'bush' out over the ground.

By the time you've finished reading this book and have followed my suggestions, you'll not only have the healthiest horses in the area, but the prettiest muck heap as well! Plant your nasturtiums on the... you guessed... muck heap.

Nasturtiums are brilliant for keeping a horse's coat in good condition. They are ideal for a horse that is changing its coat or is out of sorts.

Above Nasturtium   *Right Sage*

Staring coats caused through illness can be transformed by feeding nasturtiums. For a horse with a staring coat feed a stem, including the leaves (and flowers if possible), once a day for one week, and you should start to see a marked improvement. Horses that are out of sorts should be fed every other day at the same rate for a week. If you are giving cod liver oil as well, you will reap the benefits sooner.

For all you gourmet chefs, try adding nasturtiums to your salad, they give it colour and flavour.

SAGE

Sage comes in several forms, well two to my knowledge (someone out there is bound to prove me wrong!). The two varieties are known as white sage and red sage and have similar properties. Both varieties have dull dark green lance like leaves. But whilst one variety is tinged white the other has a reddish - purple hue. Sage is common to many gardens and patios, and you should have no problems finding it at all. This is a herb I have not in truth used very often until recently. Having just set up a new Equine Dental Surgery with a good friend of mine, I am finding it more and more useful. Basically we use it as a mouthwash after dental work.

Soak half a dozen crushed leaves in a pint of warm water for half an hour. Then using a syringe wash out the horse's mouth. This will help to alleviate sore mouths and mouth ulcers.

You will also find sage is quite effective at reducing anxiety in horses, it will also help bad travellers by helping to reduce excessive sweating. Put a couple of leaves in the horse's mouth for him to chew.

This herb should never be given to pregnant mares, as it can trigger oestrus, resulting in abortion.

STINGING NETTLES

Nettles are common plants throughout the land. They are dark green and very prolific. The leaves are almost diamond shaped with saw tooth edges.

How we all love these lovely plants ! I know, but they do have their uses. In fact try them yourself, they make a tasty side vegetable and, for

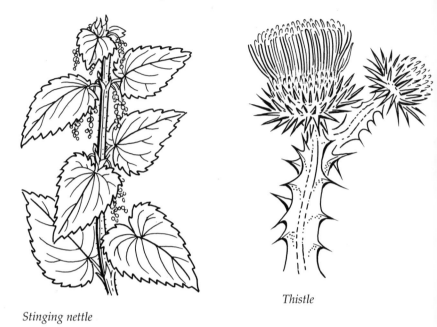

Thistle

Stinging nettle

those with the inclination, very potent beer (it's been known as the poor man's champagne).

For horses with anaemia or any form of blood disorder, stingers are a must! I personally use nettles all the time; they say prevention is better than cure!

Nettles can be administered in several ways, the first and simplest is to cut the nettles and allow them to dry. When they are 'crisp' feed them to your horse. Once again you can give as many as you like. You will be surprised how your horse will relish the taste.

In serious cases of anaemia chop, and boil the nettles until soft. It doesn't take long, they cook at the same speed as spinach. Pour the cooled liquid on to the horse's normal feed ration, adding the nettles themselves as well. You should aim to have approximately one pound of cooked nettles, and this should be fed once a day until improvement is evident.

Stinging nettles lose their sting when cooked, and I'm sure you will only need to try once before learning to judge the finished product! By the way, for the children among you remember this - nettles don't sting November! But they do sting you ! It has caught me out once or twice.

THISTLES

Prickly little blighters, but well worth the effort. Thistles are found just about everywhere you don't want them. Those picked at the roadside should be washed thoroughly before being given to your horse.

I use just the flower heads, your horse will love them. For those of you who are really keen, by stripping the outer layer and removing the thorns, you can use the whole plant.

The best thistle to use is the common thistle which has a purplish flower-head. Thistles keep well if you store them in a brown paper bag in a cool dry place.

Thistle heads are really good for the coat, especially fillies when shedding their winter coats. This applies to colts and geldings as well but seems to have a more dramatic effect on fillies.

There are no hard and fast rules as to the amount you should feed, but as a yardstick, six to twelve heads each day for a week or two are normally enough. For general use in horses with scurfy coats, feed six heads per day for a week. This amount should show a marked improvement. The bloom should start to come back in the coat. To restore your horse's coat to its full glory will of course take a little time, and grooming must form an important part of this treatment.

Should you find no improvement in the condition of your horse's coat after a week, add an extra tablespoon of cod liver oil to the feed daily. You should be feeding cod liver oil as part of the course anyway.

WILD CRESS: COW CRESS

Wild cress grows in most streams and you will notice how clear the water is after 'passing through' the cress. It is bright green with leaves similar to those of the ash tree, it has thick, hollow, rounded stems that pop when pulled. The plant has white spindly roots similar to those of mentha aquatica. Wild cress is easily administered as horses love it, but

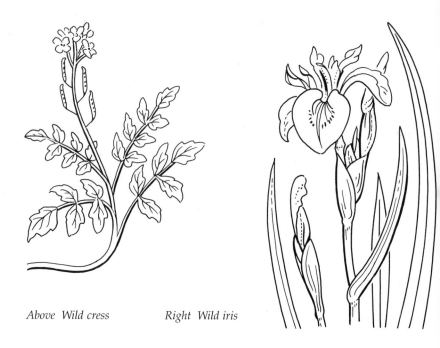

Above Wild cress   *Right Wild iris*

you must wash the plant thoroughly before feeding to remove any exterior impurities.

For general use wild cress is excellent. I have noticed that, when fed on this plant, the horse's coat always improves in condition and if I have a horse with a staring coat this is one of the first things I use. Wild cress has great restorative powers and is excellent for the convalescing horse. It will also help to build up the white blood cell count. It should be noted by those with racehorses that this can be counter productive when taking blood samples, as it can give a false impression.

You can literally feed as much of it as you like. In fact, if it is available in large quantities you can substitute it for hay during convalescence.

As with many of the cures in this book, I can offer no explanation as to why they work and, quite frankly neither could the 'old boys' who were kind enough to pass on these skills over the years. It seems to bring forth a universal answer ," Works boy doesn't it?", when the question of 'how' or 'why' is asked. I can only pass that answer on to you!

WILD IRIS, OR YELLOW FLAGS

Wild iris has thick dull, green, lance like leaves and a round flower stem (when in flower) which supports a large, yellow petalled flower. Wild iris tends to grow in thick clumps which can be found in meadows and around ponds, rivers, and streams.

The whole plant is of use, though horses do not particularly like the taste and it is very hard to get them to eat it. Wild iris should be used for blood disorders and infection.

For blood disorders, feed one small root (thoroughly cleaned) with three or four leaves daily for one week. If this fails to produce effective results, add five stalks of dried nettles, and one small plant of mentha and feed for a further five days. This will help to put any imbalances in your horse's blood back to normal.

For infections, for example, from cuts which have turned septic use the same dosage levels as above but feed as standard two to three stalks of dried nettles. Make sure you use common nettles, and not the flowering variety.

Wild iris is best chopped and added to food. I personally put it, chopped, in a bucket of barley meal in order to coat the plant liberally. I then mix it in with the horse's normal ration. Sugar beet is used as the base for all my horses' rations, the molasses helps the barley meal to disguise the taste of the plant, making it more tempting for the horse.

YELLOW TANSY

Yellow tansy has a small yellow flower head and is often found by ponds and streams (though not as often now as we would like). For Scottish readers please do not use ragwort, as I am told that in certain parts of Scotland tansies are confused or even known as ragwort. If you are at all uncertain, ring me or consult an expert in your area.

When you dig up your flower border, don't throw your tansies away! Keep them. They make an excellent fly repellent. You can either rub them directly on to the horse or crush them to make a liquid. You can if you wish, soften them in a saucepan of hot water before crushing as this makes it a lot easier to get the juices. If you use this or one of the other treatments in this book in conjunction with cod liver oil (with garlic), your horse should have no fly problems at all. Don't forget these will help to prevent Sweet Itch developing in susceptible horses and will save you a fortune on expensive remedies.

You have no excuse for running out of yellow tansy juice as it can be bottled and kept in a cool dark place for later use.

Yellow tansy

Out of the Kitchen and Into the Stable

BANANAS

Bananas contain high levels of natural sugar which are easily absorbed into the bloodstream, thus making them a very good source of energy. Being so rich an energy source, bananas are very good for horses convalescing from such illnesses as pneumonia. Bananas are also good for muscle tone and for regulating the blood.

It is far too easy to ignore a mare that is being pulled down by a foal. Feeding bananas to mares with a foal at foot will help to keep them in good condition. The role of the banana is not yet over; it has one more important part to play. It is invaluable for horses suffering from diarrhoea, as it will help significantly to 'bind' the horse up. But be careful not to feed too many bananas as they may cause colic and constipation.

Giving a horse a banana is not that easy as not many horses will accept a banana readily. Whilst fresh bananas give the best result, the simplest way is to feed dried bananas which have a sugary coating.

Suckling mares can be offered a banana once every three days. Chop the banana into small pieces and mix with the normal feed.

For competition horses, give one banana about two hours before the event. This should increase performance.

Convalescing horses can be fed one banana every two days and, for horses with digestive problems (diarrhoea) one small banana once a day for five days. If after two full days there is no marked improvement, refer to the problem chart in this book and use a different remedy. Bananas may also help, so I'm told, to increase cell counts, although this has yet to be proved.

BLACKBERRIES

The easiest way to harvest these is to pick one for you one for the horse! Blackberries can, of course, be frozen so collect as many as you can. If you don't use them for your horse, you can always make a blackberry crumble.

I am not going to insult your intelligence by telling you where to find them, but I will give a word of warning. Please make sure you wash them before feeding them to your horse as they can become contaminated by vehicle fumes etcetara. Blackberries are of use as a tonic in convalescing horses. They are a good source of energy, so have great value as a tonic. Like the fruit, the stem and leaves also have mild pain relieving qualities.

If you decide to use the stem, you must be prepared to strip the outer layer, taking any thorns as well. It isn't that the thorns will not be eaten by your horse- they probably will- but a thorn that lodges in the gums, oesophagus, palate or tongue can cause a nasty infection. The very top of the shoot is also good, especially as the thorns there have not usually hardened, and can be fed as picked.

Blackberries can be used as a 'cordial', by crushing the fruit and diluting with water. I recommend one pint of water to half a pound of blackberries. This should be fed once a day over a five day period. Never feed your horse more than half a pound of blackberries at one time, or for a period of more than five days. If your horse's dung becomes loose during this period, feed blackcurrants with the blackberries, at the dosage of four ounces of blackcurrants to half a pound of blackberries.

One word of warning, blackberries can in some horses cause a change in activity. A lazy horse may sometimes become very active and keen. If this happens, you would be well advised to use one of the other remedies suggested in this book. Your horse will come to no harm but you may find yourself disappearing over the nearest hill at high speed!

BLACKCURRANTS

It isn't often you see a horse with a sore throat! So you won't be surprised to find that this remedy is not for that particular problem! Blackcurrants are brilliant, having several uses. They can assist horses that roar or whistle, they help to inhibit bacteria such as E coli. They are also anti-inflammatory, helping muscle strains and joint problems. Blackcurrants are high in vitamin C which improves iron absorption. All in all, a miraculous little berry!

Feeding however is not always that simple as the majority of horses do not take readily to the taste. The easiest way to tempt your horse is to mix a little sugar with the berries and feed in a small bowl. This is a bit messy but it does work. If you are pushed for time I suggest you fall back on the old method of mixing the berries with the food. Be vigilant and look carefully in the corners of the bucket or trough as the little devils have a habit of spitting them out. If they do, you'll just have to try the sugar treatment.

There are no hard and fast rules when feeding blackcurrants, though one should be sensible. Don't try feeding your horse a diet of blackcurrants full stop. If you work on the premise that the intake of a 16 hh horse when being treated, should not exceed half a pound of blackcurrants per day for one week and a 12 hh pony four ounces for the same period, you can work out the dosage for all sizes.

For prevention, feed two ounces of blackcurrants every three days. For horses with back problems, feed one ounce of blackcurrants daily; this you will find helps your horse immeasurably.

BUTTER

Butter or margarine is very good for relieving colic symptoms. I really don't need to write too much on this, as it is so simple. If your horse is showing symptoms of colic put half a pound of butter or margarine in the horse's mouth and hold closed until it is swallowed. That's it! Oh! One more thing I forgot to say, have a shovel handy! As you will gather, this remedy is also very good for constipation.

CRANBERRIES

Cranberries are very useful in preventing and fighting urinary tract and kidney infections. Be sure you use either fresh cranberries, or cranberry juice with no added sugar. Fresh cranberries must be mixed with food. When I use juice, I simply pour it over the horse's feed.

As a preventative measure the juice should be given every other day at the rate of half a pint. The size of horse is fairly irrelevant, but if you are dosing a small pony it won't hurt to save a little by halving the dose.

As a remedy, fresh cranberries should be added to the feed at the rate of two ounces per day for a week. If there is no improvement, increase the dose to four ounces a day for a further week (this however, should not be necessary, as improvement should be seen within the week).

Cranberry juice should be given at the rate of one pint per day for a week, then a half pint per day for a further week.

EGGS

I have experimented on using hen's eggs to settle nervous horses and to help muscle development. Free range eggs are without doubt the best, but you can use duck, geese, ostrich, in fact any egg at all. Eggs can be fed cooked or raw, although horses take to the taste better if cooked.

Eggs in my experience have a settling effect on nervous horses when given in moderation.

If you decide to feed eggs hard boiled, the horse should be given one every other day (4 eggs in 7 days) for the first three weeks. For the next three weeks, half the dose (2 eggs in 7 days) and for a final three weeks feed just one egg a week. This regime should help to quieten nervous or upset horses. In any case, by this time you should have won the trust of the horse and settled it through constant handling ! If the horse remains nervous, stop the treatment and refer to honey.

Eggs have an extremely high protein content which is an essential part of any animal's diet. As with most things, however, too much of a good thing is not always good, so don't overdo it. Eggs fed as mentioned above are very good for building muscle in competition horses. For this use, feed one egg every three days. Do not continue this treatment longer than the stated period above.

Those with show horses will find eggs invaluable for putting a gloss in the horse's coat, but I prefer the use of cod liver oil for this purpose.

Eggs should not be fed to horses suffering from any form of osteoporosis, as they may aggravate the symptoms.

HONEY

Honey is an odd substance and I have never really got to the bottom of it. Some used to tell me honey was a mild relaxant, whilst others told me it was an energy giver. I have used it for both, even though this may seem a contradiction. Honey given as a relaxant seems to work whilst leaving the horse energised. Perhaps this is because it relaxes the horse, making it more tractable, yet doesn't affect the performance. I really don't know. All I can say is that it has always appeared to work for my horses. As an example, I recently halter-broke a very wild filly. She was stubborn to the point of being belligerent and definitely did not wish to co-operate. I took what would amount to a tablespoon of honey in my hand pushed it in her mouth, wiped the residue on the front of her lips and left her for an hour. She was, after an hour, still full of energy but was much easier to deal with. After fifteen minutes, she was actually lunging quite happily and she'd only had the halter on for two hours. Whether this was the honey, or me being a better horseman than I thought I was, I can't say, but I'm inclined to lean towards the former.

Honey is also great when trying to get a horse to take the bit for the first time. All you have to do is smear the bit with honey and you will find the horse takes it much more readily.

You will find that a spoonful of honey can also be used to hide a multitude of nasty tasting things you are attempting to get your horse to accept. It may also be added to the horse's ration, at the rate of one tablespoon a day, to help build them up, or to give them that extra bit of energy.

MUSTARD

Good old English mustard is what you need. Mustard is excellent for drawing infection out of the foot. You can either make up your own by buying the powder and mixing it with vinegar and water until it is a paste, or buy it ready made. Mixing your own is preferable. Simply paint it on the affected area of the foot and leave it on for around two hours, wash off and repeat this twice daily. You shouldn't need to do this more than two days running before you see results.

Mustard can also be used to discourage crib-biters. You need to use vinegar to mix the powder (ready made is no good for this remedy), make the mustard into a firm paste and paint on the main areas that are being bitten by your horse. They will soon get the idea that it is not a pleasant habit. If you find your horse is crib-biting another part of the stable, simply repeat the procedure, until the horse realises that, wherever he bites, you will soon follow with the mustard.

POTATOES

Apart from making great chips, I use the potato to clean wounds. Potatoes aid healing and clean the wound (this tip was passed on to me from my uncle who used to show bulls). Try it on yourself but watch out – potatoes sting, so mind you don't get kicked when treating your horse!

Cut the potato in half and rub the exposed centre on the wound. You will find this helps to stop the entry of infection into the wound site, cleans the wound, speeds the healing process and prevents scarring. Only use potatoes on small wounds such as grazes. For more serious wounds and infections, see tea tree oil.

TURNIPS

There's an old Dorset song about a chap called Buttercup Joe that my late Uncle Arthur used to sing. It's all about hoeing a field of turnips and it being the best job out. Personally I could never see the attraction, I much preferred the second verse where Buttercup Joe met the milk maid! But we won't go into that.

Turnips do have a valued use. They are quite pleasant to eat, make excellent soup and are nice roasted. More importantly they can be made into what is said to be a syrup but is in fact a watery liquid. This can be given to horses to relieve bronchial disorders and to help breathing. Used for competition horses, it will aid respiration if given in the feed.

To make the syrup, cut a medium sized turnip into pieces and boil in a small amount of water, just enough to cover the vegetable. Boil until the turnip is soft. Cool, then add both the turnip and the liquid to the horse's normal feed. You'll be surprised at the difference it makes. For those of you who compete in long distance riding, this is a must, and it's not half bad for the racehorse boys either.

Travellers' Tips

BICARBONATE OF SODA

Please don't skip through this bit as it is not just the bicarb that is important. Bicarb is one of the best cures and alleviators of laminitis. It is simple to use and cheap and easy to administer. Most horses that succumb to laminitis do so through too much grass, or obesity caused through over-eating. However, horses in poor condition have been known to contract laminitis. So it is worth considering if your horse shows signs of lameness, regardless of its condition.

Assuming your horse has laminitis caused by over- indulgence in the green stuff or the feed bin, it is important that you first cut the ration. Bran mashes are the most popular way to restrict feed intake, whilst keeping the horse happy. I will deal with that first. However, I prefer to feed from the outset and this is my personal recommendation. So, please, before you decide on a treatment, read all the information below *thoroughly*.

If you are going to feed a mash add a minimum of two tablespoons of bicarb to the bran. Mix in the normal manner with water until all the bran is well wetted, and feed. Keep your horse on this diet, plus hay (try to restrict your horse's hay to two flaps i.e. 4-5.lbs per day maximum, ponies should only be getting one flap, about 2 lbs). After a week your horse should show signs of improvement and you can then start to think about giving a low energy feed as well. Don't make the mistake of looking into those big brown eyes, and thinking, 'Well just a bit of food won't hurt' It will! Stick to the programme, even if it means you have to continue for a little longer than a week. It really is best for your horse in the long run. See the aromatherapy section, and basket willow for pain relief as well.

As I mentioned my preference is to use Alfa A, rather than bran. There are several reasons for this, the main one being that not only do I prefer Alfa A, but bran can inhibit the absorption of calcium which in effect compounds the problem. Alpha is rich in digestible fibre, and has a low sugar content. I would suggest that a horse or pony prone to laminitis be kept permanently on a base diet of light/high fibre Alfa A.

Alfa A has good protein content and is high in calcium. Alfa A can be substituted for hay or fed as a mixer. This will ensure your horse does not bolt its food, ensuring the production of saliva, important for healthy digestion.

Food intake is paramount when dealing with laminitis. Once again you must not succumb to the hungry look. Feed only to the amount of work as this will help to avoid laminitis in the first place. This applies to horses convalescing from lamintis, and to those who are prone to this problem in the first place.

For that reason, I would recommend that for a period of five days, or until your horse shows signs of improvement, you feed no more than one scoop of base feed such as Alfa A. My scoops are about six inches by five inches, and three inches deep. This can be increased when the horse shows signs of recovery. This is another product I have trialled personally, and I should add that I have been so impressed I now feed it as the standard base for all my horses' diets.

Please remember you must only feed to the horse's work load. Fat horses are unhealthy horses. As an aid to the above, I suggest the horse's feet be hosed for twenty minutes a day, or, if you are fortunate enough to have a stream or river handy, let the horses stand in the water for the same amount of time. This will help to relieve the discomfort and assist the healing process. Whatever feed you decide on, don't forget basket willow, the recommended oils (applied after the hosing or visit to the stream) and most important the bicarbonate of soda.

In my opinion, bicarbanate of soda has another use as a blood balancer. I was always told it was a great 'blood cooler', and I believe it has a valuable role for racehorses and horses in competition. Azoturia, or 'tying-up', is becoming more and more of a problem in this age of competitive sport. The greater the prizes, the more strain that the horse is put under and the more prevalent this problem will become. Bicarb may not be the be-all and end-all of the problem, but it will certainly help. It is so easy, it takes no effort at all. Just a tablespoon in the feed once a day will make all the difference. Those with race and endurance horses will find it improves the work load accepted by their horse.

Bicarb is also very good for digestive disorders. It is easier to administer bicarb dissolved in water, so dissolve a tablespoon.

One other use for bicarb (he's a versatile little chap), is as an eye wash. For both knocks and conjunctivitis, a solution of 10g bicarb per 10ml of boiled, cooled, water should be made up and the eye bathed gently twice a day. If no improvement is seen within twenty four hours, you should contact your vet. Please do not use cotton wool to bathe eyes as strands of the cotton wool can go into the eye causing further irritation.

BRIMSTONE AND LARD

Sounds a bit drastic, doesn't it, but it isn't. Mix a pound of lard - it must be lard not dripping- with a handful of brimstone (sulphur). When you have mixed it thoroughly, apply the paste to the affected areas. Again this is an old fashioned treatment, and there are remedies that offer the same protection, and are easier to use. What is it for, I hear you cry! Protection against Sweet Itch, and fly infestation.

CHALK

Wonderful stuff. You can let the little people in your life run riot and pretend to be budding Picassos, or you can work wonders for your horse. Chalk is calcium carbonate, an essential part of your horse's diet. It helps in the prevention of such injuries as splints, sore shins, even diarrhoea.

First, let us deal with the prevention bit. This should be of special interest to the racing fraternity. When you're walking through your field and you see a lump of chalk, pick it up, and take it back to the feed store. The messy part comes next. Crush the chalk by whatever means to hand. I normally use a hammer and, after putting the chalk in a tray, I give it a good whack. When it is crushed, I add a teaspoon to the normal feed. This should be done once every three days, mixing the chalk in well – and that's it.

For horses that have an existing problem, double the dose until such times as it has cleared up. You will, however need to use one of the other treatments for this as well. I would suggest you refer to comfrey, as the chalk will complement this. For horses suffering from diarrhoea, add three tablespoons of chalk to the feed to complement one of the other cures listed in this book. There are several to choose from, so you'll have to read it all now! Do not over-indulge your horse. Over feeding of chalk can cause minor problems, so please, for your own and your horses sake, follow the recommended levels.

CIDER VINEGAR

I use this purely for cosmetic reasons, and this part will be of special interest to those who wish their horses to look pristine for a show or similar. When you wash your horse down, put about a quarter of a pint of cider vinegar in with the shampoo bucket, or the rinsing water, wash the horse down as usual and you will have to wear sunglasses its coat will gleam so brightly.

Cider vinegar will help keep the flies away, but as it is not the most effective fly repellent, it would be best to look at one of the other suggestions in this book.

Cider vinegar is also used to condition a horse. Half a pint should be added to the feed, once a week. I must admit, I do not use this particular remedy so cannot comment on its effectiveness. However, that is no reason for it to be omitted.

CHIMNEY SOOT

Another old travellers remedy. They're all coming out now! Chimney soot is used to clean wounds and to reduce scarring. It is an old cure and it does work very well. However, I have only included it in this book so that it does not become lost in the mists of time. I would suggest that it be used only when no alternative is available. The best treatment for open wounds can be found in the Aromatherapy section (page 53). If you do apply this chimney soot, be vigilant as it stings a bit. Do not use on a grey horse as it may leave a mark on the skin.

COBWEBS

Cobwebs are something you should collect rather than destroy. Horses that have digestive problems can frequently be aided by the administration of cobwebs. This is I must say not the easiest of treatments to administer! Quite often a horse that has been ill, is ill or is stressed for some reason will react through its digestive system. If a horse's dung is loose, roll one *old* cobweb into a small ball, the dirty old cobwebs in the corner of the stable are best. Hold the horse's head and place the cobweb in the horse's mouth, ensuring that the cobweb is swallowed. This has remarkable results, and should 'firm' your horse up within hours. Continue with this treatment for five days only. If after this time your horse is still loose, consult the 'problem finding' chart at the end of the book, and have a word with your vet.

Cobwebs are also useful in wound healing. They are not a substitute for stitches, and should only be used on small wounds. You need a clean cobweb: a newly spun one is best, which means getting up early (dawn is the best time). Place the cobweb over the wound and bandage. Remove the bandage after 24 hours leaving the cobweb in place. Should the wound weep on removal of the bandage, place another cobweb over the existing one, but there should be no need to re-bandage the site. Not only will the cobweb assist the healing process but it should help to prevent any proud flesh developing during the healing process. For those of you who own smallholdings and have calves, cobwebs are a superb cure for scouring.

COLD TEA

If you drink as much tea as I do you will struggle to find any that's allowed to go cold. Tea is excellent for Sweet Itch. There are several remedies in this book, which are effective, but tea is one of the best. Not only does it work but it is also cheap, being a natural by-product of the kitchen. All you have to do is keep any spare tea from the pot or put the tea bags in a small container of water.

Horses don't take milk and sugar! I mention this as I recently suggested someone try this on their horse, and within two days they came back in a very irate state. Their horse was covered in flies. On finding out a little more, I discovered that they had made a cup of tea, three sugars, with milk, allowed it to cool, and poured it over the horse. When the liquid dried, all the sugar crystallised! You couldn't see the horse for flies feasting on the dried sugar. Please don't make the same mistake. The tea should be applied to the horses neck and tail. It both relieves the itching and also acts mildly as a fly repellent. Mixed with some of the oils discussed later in this book, you will have a repellent as good, if not better, than anything you can buy.

EPSOM SALTS

Epsom salts are a very good purgative but must never be given to a horse that is dehydrated. Even for horses that are suffering from constipation, you must make sure that a good water supply is available throughout the treatment. As a purgative, it should be mixed in the food at the rate of 30 gms to his normal feed. If this does not purge your horse, repeat the dose after 24 hours, you may even increase to 45 gms in the feed. If this does not have the desired effect, I would advise leaving the horse for a further 24 hours, then try one of the other remedies in this book. If your horse is in discomfort and has not responded to the first treatment, you should consult your veterinary surgeon.

I am told that Epsom salts can also be used to 'cool' a horse though in truth I have never tried this, but the old chap who told me swears by it. I don't see that giving a 'hot' horse 10 gms every once in a while can hurt, but please only do this once a fortnight maximum. If it doesn't start to work after a couple of applications, stop.

HORSE SOUP

An old traveller's remedy, horse soup is easily made and is as cheap as you will ever get. All you need is water. Leave the water in the sunniest spot you can find and allow it to go green. I'm sure you've all looked at a trough at some stage and seen thick green water. That is exactly what you want to achieve. Replace the horse's normal water with the soup for a few hours. You will need to do this twice a week for a fortnight. This will aid recovery, and help horses experiencing blood deficiencies such as anaemia. Horse soup will also help to give a horse a real bloom to their coat. Remember that the regular water troughs should always be kept clean and filled with clean water. Horse Soup is not an excuse for neglecting this important rule of horse care.

IODINE

I know using iodine is awful. I always end up looking as if I've smoked 500 cigarettes in an hour. But if you have the sense to wear gloves, which I always seem to forget, you won't have that problem. There's a moral there somewhere! Iodine is excellent in the treatment of ringworm, for cleaning out wounds, and for disinfecting. Although I personally prefer tea tree oil for the treatment of ringworm, iodine is something that is more readily available, and something that you probably have kicking around in the dark recesses of the tack room anyway. Please be careful when using iodine, it can cause irritation in some horses. For ringworm use a piece of cotton wool, wet with iodine, there should be no need to dilute, and apply to the affected area. Do this twice daily for a week. If by this time the ringworm does not show signs of clearing, continue for a further week. This should do the trick. There has been a particularly virulent strain of ringworm recently and, if you are unfortunate enough to come across this strain, I would advise you use tea tree oil.

For minor cuts, use one part iodine to three parts water and gently clean the wound, using a piece of lint or similar. It is preferable not to use cotton wool, as this has a tendency to leave strands behind in the wound, which can cause irritation.

Iodine is also very good for the treatment of thrush. If your horse is suffering from this, wash the frog well and dry. Then using a paint brush apply neat iodine to the sole, ensuring you get in all those little nooks and crannies. Repeat this daily for a week and the problem should clear.

NEWSPAPER

Newspaper can be used in two ways: first as a poultice to draw an abscess or to warm damaged tendons, secondly to keep your horse warm. As a poultice, wrap the newspaper around the affected area and bandage. You must make sure that any open wounds are covered with clean lint before applying the newspaper. Leave for twelve hours, remove and re-apply as before, making sure the area has not become too hot. You should aim to create a comfortable heat. Repeat the process for three days by which time you should have drawn the abscess.

In the case of a tendon or joint damage you should first refer to the aromatherapy section and apply oils as instructed. Then apply the newspaper for twelve hours. Remove and hose down with cold water, allow to dry, then re-apply the oils, newspaper and bandage. Repeat this for three days, then hose the leg for twenty minutes every day for a week. See comfrey, as you should with a tendon injury be giving comfrey. For horses suffering from chills or for a convalescing horse, newspaper is invaluable. Place the newspaper over the neck, back and rump of the horse. I tape the newspaper in place with masking tape and use a rug or blanket to cover. Change the newspaper everyday. This will help to keep your horse warm. He can help himself by using his energy for recuperation, rather than to produce heat. Racing boys should make a note here: you can use newspaper instead of duvets to keep your horse warm.

SALT

Just a quickie this one. Every three months I put a small handful of salt in my horses' feed. I believe this not only helps keep my horses in good condition but also helps my worming programme. None of my horses have worms so I can only say try it. Horses must have clean, fresh water available at all times.

Salt is also very good as an eye wash. Put a teaspoon of salt in about a quarter of a pint of water, and irrigate the eye. This is very good for a horse that has had a foreign body in the eye, or has weepy eyes due to dusty conditions. Horse's eyes are important and must be cared for carefully. As a cleaner of wounds, salt is excellent. Use a weak solution of one teaspoon to a pint of cooled boiled water to wash out any dirt.

Finally, mix a tablespoon of salt in a pint of warm water and use to wash off stable stains. It works really well especially on grey horses.

STOUT

If you ever visit us and we're behaving strangely, you'll know why! All stouts act as a tonic. They will 'pick up' a poor horse and help to replace any weight loss. Mind you, you should not feed more than half a pint a day, otherwise you'll find that instead of riding off into the sunset, it's more of a stagger! Stout will help keep a pregnant mare in good condition, but make sure you check your foaling dates, and stop the stout three weeks before the foaling date. If you find your horse starts to behave badly, or looks to the next drink, stop the treatment, send all your stock to me and I will look after it for you!

SUGAR AND IVY

Here I am, calling you sugar and I hardly know you!

Sugar and ivy is an old traveller's remedy and has been used as the basis of an eye wash for many years. It is quite an effective remedy and will aid in clearing up conjunctivitis. Personally, I prefer salt water washes, but nonetheless sugar and ivy washes do work. Crush a piece of ivy about ten inches long, including the leaves, place in a bowl and add a teaspoon of sugar. Pour boiling water into the bowl and allow to stand until cool, then bathe the eye with the mixture. Again, use lint rather than cotton wool for this. If you see no marked improvement within two days consult your vet.

TOBACCO

I am concerned about using prepared wormers on a regular basis.

Resistance by bacteria can build up through the over use of drugs, and I see no reason why worms should be any different. It doesn't make sense to feed worms rather than your horse. For this reason, I have through the years used prepared wormers as a supplement rather than a first defence. I must point out, before the companies producing wormers send a hit-man to silence me, that I do use wormers on occasion.

There is a small bone of contention over which brand of tobacco is best. As I write this, a traveller friend of mine is sitting with me, and we have just discussed this remedy. I prefer to use Golden Virginia or Old Holborn. He insists you should use Black or Brown Shag. I'll leave the choice up to you. It's so simple to administer. Just roll a small ball of tobacco, about the size of your small finger nail, and put in your horses mouth, making sure it is swallowed. I do this about three times a year, and worm with a prepared wormer once, or in extreme worm cases, twice a year. Tobacco is an extremely efficient wormer, but caution must be taken. Under no circumstances must the dose levels be exceeded. Tobacco can be dangerous in larger quantities.

WASHING BLUE

Another excellent wormer is old fashioned Washing Blue. This is unfortunately difficult to obtain. If you can find an old fashioned Ironmonger, ask him. Somewhere on his shelves he'll probably have some. It must be Washing Blue tablets, and definitely not a modern alternative such as Persil or Ariel. Washing Blue is the size of a 50p piece – half crown for those who remember real money – round and is about half an inch thick. Normally it is wrapped in a small cotton sack, though sometimes in paper. Put the Washing Blue in your horse's water trough, and fill with fresh water. Leave the tablet in the trough for a week, topping up the water daily as usual. After a week, remove the tablet and store it for the next time you wish to use it. You will need to do this around three times a year, substituted with one prepared wormer once a year. I must admit that I rely more on tobacco these days, as I find Washing Blue hard to obtain. Washing Blue gets white tails really white. Try it and see.

Omnipotent Oil

Cod liver oil has been used for generations and is probably well known to you. That does not mean it should be ignored. All of my racehorses, stallions and pleasure horses are kept on a course of cod liver oil. It is important in keeping the joints supple or 'well oiled' as my old mentor would say. It is well worth the expense of having a supply in your tack room and making good use of it. Cod liver oil is of great value to horses with arthritis, especially when used with other remedies such as comfrey.

Cod liver oil and associated products – I'm about to name drop here – are most important, as I will explain. First the name drop. Seven Seas who produce the Super Solvitax range are in my opinion the best on the market. I have carried out extensive independent trials of their cod liver oil, and have always found them to be of great help when I have made enquiries, no matter how obscure. For this reason I would stick to the old adage, you get what you pay for. Super Solvitax may not be the cheapest range of oils on the market, but in my opinion it is the best. If you care for your horse, then you have no excuse to cut corners in this area. Because I have been so impressed with the Super Solvitax range, I have assisted in the formulation of a new product range. Right, what does it do? I have avoided being technical so far in this book, but for this part I'm afraid you'll have to put up with a little high tech waffling.

The supplementation of cod liver oil in your horse's diet is important, even though the effects are not always noticeable. It's all to do with omega 3 polyunsaturated fatty acids. Horses are not the most efficient digesters of feed. Compared with a cow, they digest only around 45% of the cellulose intake, as opposed to 60% in the cow. The use of cod liver oil increases the absorption of minerals and trace elements, something else you should always look to provide for your horse's health. Omega 6 polyunsaturated fatty acids contained in other Seven Seas products will also increase absorption. It has been established that Super Solvitax cod liver oil is a source of high dietary energy but does not raise blood pressure, which can happen with grain feed. It slows down the digestive process, thereby allowing time for better digestion, and increasing the absorption of nutrients. It is of great value in maintaining the overall health and welfare of your horse. In the long term it will help to protect against a plethora of problems, including ringworm, joint and bone problems and elevated blood pressure. It helps recovery from injury and improves hoof health, skin, and coat condition. It will help lactating mares, increase conception rates and aid in the reduction of nervousness. It protects against rain scald, and mud fever, increases weight gain and helps maintain good eye health. It even helps to protect against stomach infestation of bot.

You can now see why it should not be overlooked. The overall benefits of feeding cod liver oil are many. It is my opinion that supplementing a horse's diet with one of the Super Solvitax range will prove an economy rather than an added expense.

Since writing this I have been involved in formulating oils with natural extracts for Super Solvitax, and can thoroughly recommend you try the range.

The reason for my high endorsement of the Super Solvitax range is because of my own trial results, which are given briefly, as follows.

REPORT: THE USE OF COD LIVER OIL TO REDUCE THE INCIDENCE OF RAINSCALD AND MUD FEVER.

What is Rainscald/Mud Fever ? Dermatophilosis is caused by prolonged exposure to moisture. The organism *Dermatophilus congolensis* gains entry through the skin when it is saturated by constant rain. Lesions are seen on the back, belly and lower limbs, causing hair loss, matting, grey green pus at the base of the hair, and skin cracking. This can lead to further infection.

FEEDING LEVELS.

I carried out this trial on a total of thirteen horses, which were split into four groups.

GROUP A. 3 horses receiving no cod liver oil supplement. Hardy types used to living out.

GROUP B. 3 horses receiving 25ml per day. Mildly susceptible, used to living out.

GROUP C. 3 horses receiving 50ml per day. Higher than average susceptibility, normally stabled during the night, but for the purposes of this trial were out 24 hrs.

GROUP D. 4 horses receiving 100ml per day. 95% susceptibility. These four horses are normally stabled during the winter. All suffer from Rainscald/Mud Fever in varying degrees. Turned out for the purposes of this trial.

Time scale: 6 months. Late autumn/early winter, and late winter/early spring.

Trial conditions   A high incidence of rain made for ideal trial conditions. With global warming on the increase, it is worth noting that the incidence of rain will become greater.

RESULTS

GROUP A.
None of the three horses in this group had previously shown any susceptibility to Rainscald or Mud Fever. However, because of the conditions, exceptional amounts of rain, all three horses contracted both Rainscald and Mud Fever. These problems became so serious that I was forced to stable all three animals. I am now putting to the test the recuperative properties of cod liver oil for Rainscald and Mud Fever.

GROUP B

All of the horses in group B had a past history of suffering mildly from Rainscald and/or Mud Fever . Feeding 25 mls daily, reduced the problem by around 75%. The horses still showed mild symptoms of Mud Fever, but it was negligible in comparison to previous years. I considered this a marked improvement considering the level of rain.

GROUP C. The three horses who made up group C, were particularly prone to Rainscald and to Mud Fever. The severity of both conditions had in previous years caused chronic hair loss on the back and around the fetlock joints of all three. We fed 50ml cod liver oil daily. This reduced the problem to a few minor scabs on the area around the withers. The scabbing was so minor that it created no problem what so ever.

GROUP D. Normally stabled during the winter months, the horses in this group were turned out for the purpose of the trial. They were fed a high dose of 100ml cod liver oil a day. It was within this group that we saw the most spectacular results; all of the horses should have been greatly affected by Mud Fever and we had no incidence. The results amazed me.

The dosage for this group was high and I must stress that I would not ordinarily feed cod liver oil at this level. However for the purpose of this trial, we were putting the horses into a managerial situation where if they could get Mud Fever or Rainscald they would and that during the trial we were only looking at the feeding of cod liver oil.

The result was that this group of horses came out of the trial surprisingly well. None of them got Rainscald and/or Mud Fever. Not only that, but their coats and overall condition improved hugely. This can only be put down to the cod liver oil we were feeding.

CONCLUSION

Rainscald and Mud Fever are the scourge of winter. Both conditions cause great discomfort and in the case of Mud Fever sometimes lameness and because of this horses, by default lose condition.

We found that feeding cod liver oil as a supplement to standard rations proved to be of great benefit to the horses health and general condition. Not only did the trial show that cod liver oil reduces the occurance of Mud Fever, but it also improves digestion, thus enhancing condition. Although cod liver oil is quite expensive, it is false economy not to feed it and in my view, the cost is more than offest in the improved condition you will see in your horses.

Rubbing it In

Girls, you'll love it, not only will the horses smell divine, but you won't have much difficulty talking the lads into giving you a quick rub down!

Aromatherapy has been around for centuries. The Chinese, Australian Aborigines and Ancient Egyptians all relied heavily on the use of oils as curatives. To my mind, aromatherapy is one of the most ignored methods of treating horses, but for me it is a method of treatment I prefer to use wherever possible.

Aromatherapy is the application of Essential Oils. You must not confuse these with scented oils. *Essential oils must be specifically for application by massage* so please take care when buying your oils. By mixing oils with a base oil, (I always use sweet almond oil for a base) it is amazing what you can achieve.

Mixing is easy. All you need is a bottle, preferably dark in colour as bright light will reduce the potency of the oils, the oils themselves, and a base oil. You will find that the horses enjoy being treated and also seem to be fascinated by the smell of the oils. The only difficulty you may encounter is to keep their noses from getting in the way. Before we go into the oils themselves, you need to know the basic massage techniques, and so I will concentrate on these first. Practise them on a member of your family or a friend. Enjoy.

Point to remember

I have found that you can safely mix most oils, and will have no problems mixing the oils listed in this book. But you must not mix more than three or four maximum, in desperate cases, and you must always remember to use a carrier oil (such as sweet almond or grape).

BASE OILS

Aloe vera: Is a plant based gel which must be used in a pure form. I use a pure gel which is very effective, and is good as it leaves little or no residue at all. Go to a reputable outlet to purchase it.

Coconut: A light oil which is readily absorbed and leaves little residue. Excellent for all mixes.

Sweet almond oil: can be used as a base for any of your mixes, though it is best used when you are dealing with a leg problem. It is very good when treating mud fever as it is fairly heavy and helps to protect the site from moisture. Sweet almond oil is a good all rounder, although for cosmetic reasons I now use a lighter oil such as coconut or white lotion on highly visible areas of skin.

White lotion: Available from Amaranth (see useful addresses). I find myself using more and more of this as my base. It really is good.

MASSAGE TECHNIQUE

The only difference between the technique used on horses and on ourselves is the amount of pressure applied. Horses are much stronger than we are so it is important that enough pressure is applied when using aromatherapy for muscle and skeletal applications. Wounds, fungal infections, inhalations, skin problems, etc. do not require massage, which you will learn as you read on. First let us deal with the amount of pressure to apply. For ease I will list these as 1, 2 and 3. If you try this on yourself, you will soon get the knack.

No.1 is a deep massage, usually used for muscular injuries. Put the flat of your hand against the top of your thigh, pushing down, then, keeping the pressure on, try to slide your hand down towards your knee. You should sit in a chair for this exercise. When you find you can just keep the hand moving downwards while still holding the pressure on, you have found the correct firmness.

No.2 requires the same procedure, but with only enough pressure to 'roll' the muscle in front of your hand.

No.3 is simplicity itself. Carry out the same method as before but, this time, with only sufficient pressure to 'stroke' the skin gently.

Heat massage is achieved by moving the hands rapidly backwards and forwards. This warms the patient and the oils, which are then absorbed more quickly. Oils will carry on working on the injury for about 12 hours.

Your palm is the key to good massage. Don't take any notice of the James Bond movies, you won't need to walk bare foot along your horse's back, nor will you need to become a karate expert, and try chopping them in half ! When you are applying oils, imagine you are kneading dough to make bread: use the whole palm, the fingers, thumbs and most important of all, the heel of your hand.

Aromatherapy does not end with muscular injuries. There are applications for calming anxious horses, for alleviating stress in horses who travel poorly and even as an aid against equine herpes. You can experiment yourself by mixing oils. Aromatherapy is a very personal thing,

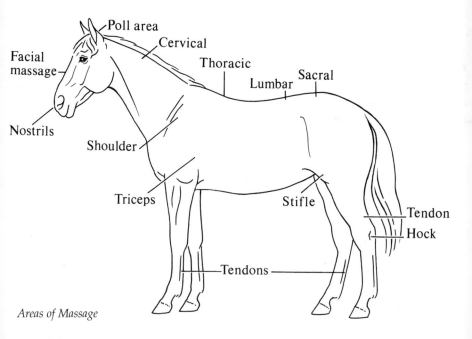

Areas of Massage

each horse reacts differently. So don't be afraid to try something out, just use ½ ml of a particular mixture, and work from there.

There are literally hundreds of oils available. I have only written on those most commonly used and most readily available. I hope I have achieved my aim to make the subject both easy to follow, and interesting. Remember practice makes perfect, so ignore the sceptics – and there are plenty of them – and keep going. It's the sceptics who will end up eating humble pie.

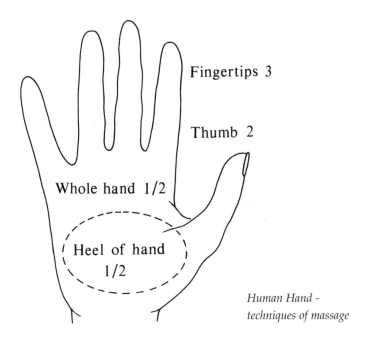

Fingertips 3

Thumb 2

Whole hand 1/2

Heel of hand 1/2

Human Hand -
techniques of massage

BLACK PEPPER

Black pepper is excellent for helping to heal tendon injuries, muscle tears and in the treatment of general muscular pain. It has, as you would expect, a strong warming effect and you will only need a small amount. Add 1 ml to a base of 10 mls sweet almond oil, then experiment, using some of the other recommended oils in this book. Apply, using massage technique 1-2, on the affected area. This will ensure that the oils are worked in to the area well.

CAMPHOR

Camphor is one oil that is really potent, and you must not use this oil on horses that have breathing problems. However it is very good for muscular strain and aches, and it is also an excellent insect repellent. To use this oil, you must make sure your horse has a paddock or yard to walk in, as it does give off strong fumes. Mix 1 ml of camphor oil with 15 mls of sweet almond oil, and apply to the affected area. I normally keep the use of this oil to leg massage, using Technique 2. This treatment must not exceed three days.

CINNAMON

Cinnamon is quite a versatile oil, and can be mixed with most other oils. I use cinnamon as a 'helper' oil, and add it to a lot of my mixes. I have also used cinnamon in conjunction with tea tree to treat bruised soles, with some success. Cinnamon is very good for horses with digestive disorders as well as for respiratory problems. You will find it helps reduce the problem of roaring.

For digestive complaints add 1 ml of cinnamon, 1 ml fennel, and 2 mls peppermint to 10 mls sweet almond oil. Apply to the lower part of the horse's belly, keeping up the once-daily treatment until such time as the horse improves.

For roarers, add 1 ml cinnamon, 2 mls eucalyptus, 1 ml lavender to 10 mls sweet almond oil and apply generously to the throat and nose area, using massage technique 3. This treatment will need to be carried out daily, and will have to become part of the horse's regular routine. Cinnamon is also excellent for muscular pain, as it will help to warm the problem area.

CITRONELLA

This is one we could not miss, though its use solely as an insect repellent is underrated. It is very good at relieving muscular pain and stiffness and can be safely mixed with some of the other, more powerful oils, mentioned in this book for muscular problems. Citronella is best avoided for pregnant mares. As an insect repellent mix 2 mls citronella in 300 ml of warm water and spray. Alternatively, you can mix 2 ml in 10 ml of sweet almond oil and apply directly to the areas most affected by this problem.

CYPRESS

Cypress is a warm woody oil, and I have found it good for bleeders, and with mares suffering from stomach cramp during season. Ask yourself why some mares get so cranky! They can suffer too, you know. Mixed with some of the other suggested oils in this book it will helps soothe your mare's discomfort. Use 2 mls in 10 mls of sweet almond oil and using Techniques 2-3 rub into the abdominal region and on the rump. For bleeders use 3 ml cypress oil in 10 ml sweet almond oil and work into the rib area: using Technique 2, apply to the neck and, with Technique 3, treat each side of the nasal bridge.

Cypress oil is also a good oil for alleviating swelling after exercise or competition. For this you should use 1 ml, mixed with compatible oils such as eucalyptus, lemon oil, or lime, in of course the obligatory 10 mls of sweet almond oil.

EUCALYPTUS

Eucalyptus originally came solely from Australia but is now grown in California, Spain and Portugal. We have to thank the Aboriginal people for the discovery of this versatile oil. In fact the oil was used extensively during the 2nd World War. Many soldiers have this oil to thank for aiding their recovery. It was this that probably brought it to the fore.

I have found eucalyptus to be most versatile and an excellent oil for mixing. Eucalyptus is the best oil to use for tendon and muscle strain, when mixed, but it also has a valuable use for other injuries. If you work on the premise of putting 1 ml of eucalyptus in all your preparations you will not go far wrong

For muscle strain, and tendon injury, work on using 2-3 mls in your mix. It is not my intention to confuse you with too many different 'recipes', and so I will concentrate on giving you the basic mixtures that I use frequently.

Tendon Injury

Mix 3 mls eucalyptus, 1 ml lime, 1 ml peppermint and 2 mls black pepper in 10 mls of sweet almond oil. It is an important part of this treatment to concentrate on the tendon area itself.

Remember to be patient, the horse will be finding it uncomfortable before the oil takes effect, and may try repeatedly to lift his leg from your grasp. Holding the leg (I find it easiest to stand with my shoulder against the horse's chest), place approximately 1 tspn of oil in the palm of your hand and gently apply to the tendon. Once the oil is covering the area apply pressure (Technique 2) with the thumb and forefinger and work the oil in well, this normally takes around five minutes. You should now have your horse feeling a little more comfortable and can apply a heat massage. This is quite tiring to do on a tendon, so make sure you apply plenty of deodorant before you start! Still using the thumb and forefinger rub the tendon with a fast up and down movement. You will actually feel the heat yourself. Do this for about two minutes. If the injury is of a fairly serious nature you should apply the treatment twice daily for at least a week. In less severe cases, once daily will suffice. After a week, you should be seeing an improvement. If this is not the case, then carry on with the treatment for a further week. The heat massage is important as it will help the oils to be absorbed more quickly, and will stimulate blood flow.

Muscle pain and stiffness

Personally, I find treating this type of problem very therapeutic myself. There is no real need to concentrate on what you are doing, and you can really let yourself become one with the horse. You will also find that as you are rubbing the oils with the palms, thumbs and heel of your hands, it will be absorbed by you. With a mixture of 2 mls eucalyptus, 1 ml lime, 1 ml cinnamon and 1 ml black pepper, the massage should be given using technique 1, and should finish on a heat massage. Use your hands to 'feel' the problem. You should, if you are following this properly, feel the knots in the horse's muscles. Work on these. To be effective, you have to try to 'smooth' the horse's muscle.

Oils can also help to alleviate stiffness caused by overwork and even old age. Use the same mixture but employ a technique between 2, 3 and heat and work on the affected area. You will also find it helpful to feed a cod liver oil, or equivalent supplement in your horse's diet. It will also help if you refer to the plants and potions section. Bit like trying to read a jack- in- the box, isn't it? Never mind, it will be worth the effort in the end.

FENNEL

If you refer back to the plant section you may be surprised to find that I use the oil for something I have not mentioned there. Fennel is excellent for mares in season. I have a mare that when in season is a real tart, so much so that we had her stitched up. Whilst this improved her in training, her demeanour was still a bit on the temperamental side. She definitely suffered from PMT! Fennel is of great use when dealing with such a mare. It helps calm the temperament, and soothes the symptoms of their season. Mix 2 mls of fennel oil with 1 ml geranium oil in 5 mls of sweet almond oil.

You can use this in several ways, and it will not hurt to go through the whole process listed. It only takes a minute more and will be that much more effective. First, use as an inhalation by holding the bottle containing the liquid about an inch from your horse's nostrils. Allow your horse to inhale for about a minute. Then use Technique 3, apply the oil to the area between but not inside the horse's nostrils. Around ½ tsp is enough, then carefully lift the tail, and apply the same amount to the underside of the dock. You can if there is any left gently rub into the back area just in front of the point of the hips. Ladies, you can use this yourselves if necessary, so it is well worth keeping these oils in stock. Fennel is also very good at alleviating digestive pain and should be used by mixing 2 mls fennel with 10 mls sweet almond oil and rubbing the mixture into the area behind the ribs and under the belly using Technique 2. Jasmine is also very good for this application, but is unfortunately very expensive which is why I have not included it in this mixture.

GERANIUM

Geranium oil does have many uses and is an important oil when performing equine aromatherapy. Geraniums are grown in Europe, Egypt, the Congo, and in Madagascar. The smell is very pleasant and you will find yourself in the strange position of wanting to return to your horse and giving it a good sniff. The oil is mildly antiseptic, and is therefore a good one to add at the rate of 1 ml to any cut mixture you make. It will also help alleviate bruising and skin problems.

If you find you have a problem with rainscald or mud fever, geranium is a must. I remind you that you should be feeding an oil additive in your feed! Mix 2 mls of geranium with 2 mls of tea tree, 1 ml of eucalyptus, plus 1 ml of lemon in serious cases, to 10 mls of sweet almond oil and apply to the affected area, using a technique between 2 and 3. Make sure that you do not just put the oil on and leave it. Work it in well. You should start to see improvement within ten days.

GINGER

Ginger is a potent oil and should not be over used. Please stick to the recommended levels, and if your horse shows any sign of adverse reaction stop the treatment and use one of the other oils. Ginger is very good for increasing the blood circulation in laminitic horses and should be applied at the rate of 1 ml per 10 mls sweet almond oil. Simply brush on to the wall of the hoof and on the sole and leave (warm the oil slightly before doing so).

It is also good for relieving fever, and for this should be applied at the same rate (one in ten), using Technique 2, to the back and chest areas. Repeat this daily until the fever abates. Once again, if any adverse reaction is seen, use one of the other oils.

JASMINE

I will not write a great deal on this oil as it is very expensive. About the same price as gold! When you consider it takes about eight million flowers to make a single kilo of oil you will understand why ! Jasmine, because of its cost, should be used as a last resort. 1 ml in 5 mls of sweet almond oil, or grape oil should be more than enough. Use it for serious cases of stress, and for mares with problems when in season. Apply as for fennel.

JUNIPER

Juniper is very versatile, but one word of warning ! You must never use this on a pregnant mare, as it may well trigger labour. Juniper can be used to relieve mare-ishness when in season, is very good for skin problems and is also a calmer. Use 1 ml in 10 mls sweet almond oil plus a selection of two other oils of your choice. By now, you should have gleaned sufficient knowledge from my words of wisdom to apply and treat the problem.

LAVENDER

If you work on the premise that each mixture you make includes a small dose of lavender – (it is an extremely safe oil), you won't go far wrong. Lavender is one of my favourite oils and is one you should make use of for yourself as well as your horse. It is good for bad travellers, nervous horses, stressed horses and as an aid in convalescing horses. In my opinion it is unbeatable. Add 5 mls of lavender, 2 mls orange and 1 ml fennel to 10 mls sweet almond oil. The fennel will help to relieve physical stress, such as upset stomach, stomach cramps and muscle cramps. Lavender is obviously the main ingredient in this mixture, but you will find the inclusion of the other two oils assists. Using Technique 3 apply the oil to the area between the nostrils, then with Technique 2 apply the oil to the neck, back, between the eyes (making sure you do not get any in the eye itself) and between the ears. Do this an hour before you wish to travel your horse and you will find that he or she is far more relaxed and does not become too stressed on the journey.

For nervous horses, use the same mixture and procedure (if you wish you can omit the fennel, though you will do no harm by adding it) just after morning feed. Repeat this daily, reducing the amount applied over a period of two weeks. You should, by this time, see a marked difference. Do not worry if your horse becomes nervous or stressed when you finish the treatment as you can reintroduce it. You can do no harm by keeping a horse on it.

If you are having trouble sleeping, or are of a nervous disposition try putting, the amount shown above in your bath. It may well surprise you.

LEMON

The zest of the lemon is gorgeous, and this oil can even be used as an air- freshener by putting a few drops on the carpet or on your radiators. Lemon is basically an invigorator, and I add it at the rate of 1 ml to many of my mixes. If you have a tired or jaded horse, use lemon oil as the base of your mix.

LIME

As you will have gathered, I use lime quite frequently. I mix it with most oils, as it has anti-bacterial and anti-viral properties. It is also an excellent tonic. If you have a jaded horse, or a horse recovering from illness, add a little lime to their lives. I am not going to bore you with mixtures, but simply advise adding 2 ml to your own mixture. By now, you should be able to work out what's best for your horse. After all, you know him or her much better than I do!

MANDARIN

Girls, you can wear this one as a perfume. It smells gorgeous! I'll throw in an extra one here. What value for money! If you have just been doing a bit of slimming and want to reduce stretch marks, this is for you. Put 7 drops in 2 tblspn of grape oil and rub in well. Avoid sunbathing whilst using this oil, as it is quite strong and if exposed to direct sunlight may cause irritation.

Right, back to the babies. Mandarin is very good for restless horses, and will help against such vices as box walking. It will in some cases also aid mares who become 'tetchy' when in season. Use $1/2$ ml in 10 mls sweet almond oil, and employing Technique 2-3, apply to the underside of the neck, belly and under the jaw line. You can if you wish, use another oil to complement, which I will leave to you, though violet, lavender or juniper are very good.

MARIGOLD

I have a mare that suffers from sunburn and cracked skin. Although she is an absolute poppet and never complains, it does make her very sore. One of the best ways to alleviate this problem is to use marigold oil. Mix 3 ml marigold and 1 ml lime with 10 mls of any of the following carriers: sweet almond, peach kernel or jojoba. For this purpose I personally prefer jojoba oil. Apply the mixture to the affected area, using Technique 3. Remember be gentle as sunburn is painful.

ORANGE

Orange is another stimulator, and should be used as lemon oil. Unlike lemon oil, it will also calm the subject at the same time. It does however have a further use which is to help skin problems. For horses with any dermatological problem, it is very good and should be used at the rate of 2 ml per 10 ml of sweet almond oil and applied to the affected area. It can, as with lemon, be used in your atomiser at the rate of 2 ml per 500 ml of warm water. Make sure you shake it up well.

PEPPERMINT

Peppermint oil is lovely to use and will fill your stable or yard with its fresh fragrance. More importantly, it is a great oil for both digestion and breathing. I also use this oil as a 'mixer' for muscle problems, as it has warming qualities.

To use peppermint oil for breathing problems, mix with eucalyptus at the rate of 1 ml eucalyptus, 3 ml peppermint to 15 ml sweet almond oil. Rub into the area on each side of the nasal bridge, the throat, and middle back. It is also as well to hold the container under the horse's nose for a few minutes for him to inhale. Peppermint oil is especially helpful to horses suffering from the after effects of colic, To use it as a digestive aid, mix 2 ml peppermint, 2 ml fennel and 1 ml lime in 15 ml of sweet almond oil. You can keep both these treatments up for as long as necessary. In horses with permanent breathing problems, it is wise to halve the amount of Essential oil, mix it with 15 ml sweet almond oil, and use every other day.

PINE

Whenever we have a horse experiencing breathing difficulties, the words of an old chap I used to help out at the horse sales always come back to me. 'Give 'im a breath of the pine, boy !' In other words, take him for a quiet walk through a pine wood. It definitely helps; you only have to go and sit in a pine wood when you have a cold to prove it. You come back mildly refreshed and far less stuffy! Pine oil comes in little bottles, so the breath of the pines can be held in your pocket! Use it for horses which are experiencing breathing difficulties. I would advise adding 2 mls to a mixture of 10 mls sweet almond oil, 2 mls eucalyptus and 1 ml peppermint. Apply between and to outer nostrils, the soft area at the side of the face, and to the lower jaw, using Techniques 2 and 3. The treatment should be carried out for a week to ten days.

TEA TREE OIL

Tea tree oil is one of my favourites and is added to 90 percent of the treatments I mix. All the oil comes from Australia and is used extensively by the Aboriginal people. Tea tree oil is a non-irritant, though it does sting a little on application. A spicy, woody smelling oil, tea tree is more than ten times stronger than carbolic at killing bacteria, and curing fungal and viral infections. Any wound can be treated with tea tree oil and, for wounds that are serious, you will find little better. It is also effective on stings, bites, ringworm and I have even had success in the treatment of warts. For an abscess of the foot, tea tree oil is extremley effective, as it is for any deep rooted infection.

VIOLET

Violet is soothing to both body and mind, and can treat skin problems and ease stress. For those of you who suffer from headaches, it will prove invaluable when used in conjunction with lavender. The next bit will probably cause a raised eyebrow or two, and probably a few giggles. I believe that horses suffer from headaches just as we do. Bit of a country cure for good measure here. Watch a horse that is showing signs of irritability, and is reluctant to have his or her head brushed or is difficult to get a head collar on. Nine times out of ten such a horse will, when turned out, go directly to something such as a blackberry bush, basket willow or the bark of a rotten tree and have a good chew. Natural aspirin, need I say more.

Violet is very good for helping this problem, which I personally do not believe should be taken lightly. Racehorse boys, take note ! It doesn't hurt to try this application on your horse an hour or two before the race! Mix 3 ml violet in 10 ml of sweet almond oil and apply, using Technique 3, to the nasal bridge and between the eyes and ears. It's that simple! The same mixture applies to those horses with localised skin complaints. Those with a more general problem, such as scurfy coat, should be treated as follows. Mix 3 ml violet, 1 ml tea tree in 500 ml warm water, then, using a small vaporiser (garden spray), spray the horse's coat liberally. Job done.

WHITE THYME

First, a piece of totally useless information that you can stun your friends with. Thyme used to be sewn into a Knight's clothing and it was purported to keep him brave during battle! So if you're riding a horse that bucks a lot in the morning, try sticking a sprig down your jodhs!

Thyme is a powerful antiseptic. It is also a good expectorant and insect repellent. I must admit I personally use it for the last two reasons. Horses experiencing coughs and colds can be helped immeasurably by this oil. Mix 1 ml thyme, 1 ml eucalyptus, 1 ml peppermint in 10 mls of sweet almond oil, and apply to the underside of the neck, using Techniques 2-3, the rib area using Techniques 1-2, and the area each side of the nasal bridge, using Technique 3. Continue this until the symptoms are relieved. As an insect repellent, simply mix 3 mls with 15 mls of sweet almond oil and apply to those areas mainly affected – face, tail, ears, belly. This mix should last you about three weeks, and should be applied once weekly.

YLANG YLANG

The bells are ringing for me and my girl... I never was much of a singer. Ylang ylang has one important property, though I have seen many different recommendations. Using ylang ylang is in my opinion specific, and I would advise against using it for anything other than that mentioned in this passage. Please read this carefully. For those with stallions (or partners that are always too tired – it works on both sexes, by the way!) - ylang ylang is the oil you need. It will give new life to stallions, and will also encourage mares to come into season, and be more tractable with the stallion. Mix 3 mls of ylang ylang in 3 mls of sweet almond oil. Dip two fingers in the mixture, apply to the fleshy area between the nostrils and using Technique 2, massage the remainder into the area just in front of the hip (central above the backbone). Leave the horse for two to three hours and your horse will be raring to go. You will also find that your horse is more relaxed and less prone to stress. You can use the same mixture for yourself, just make sure you haven't got an early start!

A quick reminder

Right, if you haven't fallen asleep (I told you to pay attention at the back!) You should by now have grasped the basics of equine aromatherapy. Mixing is easy as long you always use a good base oil, such as sweet almond, and don't get over zealous with the essential oils. You can develop your own concoctions to suit your horse. As a general rule of thumb, I always say, if it doesn't hurt you, it won't hurt your horse. So don't be afraid to try it on yourself. I have just treated one of Anne Holland's horses, Buster, a really sweet hunter with a shoulder injury. I used the same mixture on my girlfriend when she had a bad back. It worked for both of them.

Please keep your oils in dark glass bottles, out of direct sunlight, but do not take the glass bottles into your stables for obvious reasons. Use a plastic bottle or bowl when applying the oils, but always, BUT ALWAYS, return your mix to a clean dark glass bottle for storage. Oils do not keep well in plastic bottles. If you add a teaspoon of wheatgerm oil to your mixture, it has a shelf life of up to six months.

Oh, and never under any circumstances use essential oils neat. Always dilute them by adding them to a base oil. There is, however one exception to this rule – tea tree oil which may be applied directly and undiluted to Ringworm but only as a last resort.

One of the most important things to remember is that you have not become a miracle worker. You will need patience and dedication to effect repairs and you will not heal your horse overnight. Neither have you become a vet – so please, and I send this out to vets as well – give each other a chance. Don't become blinkered, and ask your vet not to, either, but do remember he is a professional and has access to many marvellous drugs. You on the other hand, have the availability of years of knowledge passed on by many great horsemasters. So work together for the good of the horse.

I hope you have enjoyed the contents of this book. Who knows, maybe we'll meet up one day at a show or something? In the meantime, my best wishes to you all, and to your sweet smelling and healthy horses.

Quick Reference Guide

Promotional products

Promoting	Herbal	Other	Aromatherapy
Anti-bacterial	Garlic	Blackcurrants	Eucalyptus Lime Tea Tree
Anti-inflammatory		Blackcurrants	
Anti-viral	Garlic		Lime Tea Tree
Antiseptic		Salt	White Thyme
Blood balance	Garlic	Bicarbonate of Soda	Garlic
Conditioning	Chives	Cider Vinegar Cod Liver Oil Dandelion Eggs Wild Cress	

Promoting	Herbal	Other	Aromatherapy
Convalescence	Water Mint	Bananas Blackberries Newspaper Stout Wild Cress	Lavender
Energy		Cod Liver Oil Honey Banana	Lemon
Healthy Coat	Chives	Cod Liver Oil Dandelion Eggs Nasturtium Thistles Wild Cress	
Lower Heart Rate	Garlic	Basket Willow	
Muscle tone		Bananas	
Relaxation	Basil		Orange
Warming		Newspaper	Lime

Treatments

Problem	Herbal	Other Cures	Aromatherapy
Abscess		Dead Nettle Newspaper	Tea Tree Oil Lavender

Problem	Herbal	Other	Aromatherapy
Arthritis	Comfrey		Eucalyptus Pine Lime
Bad Travellers	Basil Sage	Dead Nettle	Lavender
Bleeders	Water Mint	Basket Willow	Cypress
Blood Disorders	Garlic	Bananas 'Horse Soup' Wild Iris	Peppermint Garlic
Bruised Soles	Comfrey		Lime Cinnamon
Bruising	Comfrey		Lime Geranium
Chipped Knees	Comfrey		
Colds	Water Mint		White Thyme
Colic	Dill Fennel	Butter	Cypress
Conjunctivitis		Salt Sugar-and-Ivy	
Constipation		Epsom Salts	
Coughing	Water Mint		White Thyme

Problem	Herbal	Other	Aromatherapy
Cuts	Amaranth	Cobwebs Iodine	Eucalyptus Tea Tree
Dermatological disorders		Marigold Cold Tea	Violet Geranium Juniper Orange
Diarrhoea		Blackcurrant Bananas Chalk	Peppermint
Digestion	Amaranth Bananas Blackcurrants Cobwebs Fennel	Cinnamon Fennel Peppermint	
Fever			Ginger
Headaches			Lavender Violet
Impotence	Fennel		Fennel Ylang Ylang
Infection		Wild Iris Hazel	Cinnamon Eucalyptus Peppermint Pine

Problem	Herbal	Other	Aromatherapy
Insect Repellent	Chives Garlic	Marigold Yellow Tansy	Camphor Citronella Tea Tree White Thyme
Lactating mares		Fennel	
Laminitis		Bicarbonate of Soda	Ginger
Mare-ishness			Fennel
Mares in Season	Fennel		Fennel Cypress Juniper Mandarin Ylang Ylang
Mud Fever		Cod Liver Oil	Geranium
Muscular strain			Eucalyptus Black Pepper
Nervousness		Honey	Lavender
Oedema		Dandelion	
Pain		Basket Willow Blackberries Dead Nettles	Black Pepper Camphor Citronella Eucalyptus
Rain Scald		Cod Liver Oil	Geranium

Problem	Herbal	Other	Aromatherapy
Respiratory		Blackcurrants Turnips	Cinnamon Eucalyptus Peppermint Pine
Ringworm		Iodine	Lime Tea Tree
Sore Mouths	Sage		
Sore Shins	Comfrey	Chalk	Lime Eucalyptus Black Pepper Peppermint
Sores			Tea Tree Oil
Splints	Comfrey	Chalk	Eucalyptus Lime
Stable Vices		Mustard	Lavender Mandarin
Stiffness			Eucalyptus Black Pepper
Stress Fractures		Comfrey	Lime Eucalyptus Black Pepper
Stress		Basil Sage	Fennel Geranium

Problem	Herbal	Other	Aromatherapy
			Jasmine
			Lavender
			Violet
Sunburn			Marigold
Sweet Itch	Garlic	Brimstone & Lard	Tea Tree
		Cold Tea	Citronella
		Yellow Tansy	Garlic
			Lime
Swelling			Eucalyptus
			Cypress
			Lime
Tendon Strain	Comfrey	Newspaper	Pine
			Eucalyptus
			Lime
Thrush		Iodine	Lime
			Tea Tree
Ulcers	Sage		
Urinary Infections		Cranberries	
Windgalls			Lime
			Eucalyptus

Problem	Herbal	Other	Aromatherapy
Worms		Salt Tobacco Washing Blue	
Wounds	Amaranth	Chimney Soot Cobwebs Iodine Potatoes	Tea Tree Lavender Eucalyptus

Useful Addresses

ADAS (Food Farming, Land and Leisure). *see* Local Directories.

Aloe Vera Equicare.
15 Alders Road, Edgware, Middlesex, HA8 9QG.
Tel. 0181 959 2452

Amaranth
PO Box 3655
Blandford Forum
DT11 8YP
Tel. 07020 935284

British Association of Holistic Nutrition and Medicine (BAHNM).
Borough Court, Hartley Wintney, Basingstoke, Hants, RG27 8JA.
Tel. 01252 843282.

British Association of Homeopathic Veterinary Surgeons.
Alternative Medicine Centre, Chinham House, Stanford in the Vale, Faringdon, Oxon SN7 8NQ.
Tel. 01367 710324

British Veterinary Association.
7 Mansfield Street, London, W1M OAT. Tel. 0171 6366541

Complimentary Animal Therapies. 37 Tinshill Road, Cookridge, Leeds, W. Yorkshire, LS16 7DR. Tel. 0113 2301996

Equiherb. Herbal Dispensary for Horse and Rider.
103 High Streetm Syston, Leics. LE7 1GQ. Tel. 0116 2694590.

Hilton Herbs Ltd.
Downclose Farm, Downclose Lane, North Ferrott, Crewherne, Somerset, TA18 7Sh.
Tel. 01460 78300 (helpline).

Ministry of Agriculture, Fisheries and Food.
Ergon House, c/o Nobel House, 17 Smith Square, London SW1P 3RJ.

Natural Animal Feeds Ltd.
High House, Penrohs, Raglan, Monmouthshire, NP5 2DJ.
Tel. 01600 780256.

Royal College of Veterinary Surgeons.
32 Belgrave Square, London SW1 8QP. Tel. 0171 222 2001 (Membership).

Seven Seas Limited.
Hedon Road, Hull, England, HU9 5NJ. Tel. 01482 375234.

Wendals Herbs Ltd.
Westfield House, Terrington St Clement, King's Lynne, Norfolk. PE34 4EX. Tel. 01553 828111

Westminster Natural Health Centre.
52 Rochester Row, Westminster. SW1P 1JU. Tel. 0171 834 0861.

American Holistic Veterinary Association.
Dr. C. Ticket, 2214 Old Emmerton Road, Bel Air, Maryland, 21014, USA.

Herb Research Foundation.
1007 Pearl Street, Suite 200, Boulder CO 80302. USA.

National Herbalist Association of Australia.
37 Leith Street, Coorparoo, Queensland, 4151.

OTHER PUBLICATIONS AVAILABLE FROM COMPASS EQUESTRIAN:		
Title	**Price**	**Tick your order**
A Young Person's Guide to Dressage Jane Kidd	£13.95	
Focused Riding - Robert and Beverley Schinke	£12.95	
The BAHNM Dictionary of Holistic Horse Medicine and Management - Keith Allison.	£10.99	
Riding for Gold - 50 Years of Horse Trials in Great Britain - Jane Pontifex	£25.00	
Compass Pony Guide Series		
Book 1 - More Than Just A Pet	£2.99	
Book 2 - Head First	£2.99	
Book 3 - Bodywork	£2.99	
Book 4 - Forelegs and Four Feet	£2.99	
Book 5 - A Bit More Than A Mouth	£2.99	
Book 6 - Top, Tail and Overcoat	£2.99	
Book 7 - Filling Up The Tank	£2.99	
Book 8 - Why Does He Do That?	£2.99	
Compass Points for Riders Series		
1. Snaffles - Carolyn Henderson	£6.99	
2. Training Aids - Carolyn Henderson	£6.99	
3. Plants, Potions and Oils for Horses - Chris Dyer	£6.99	

P&P free

To order please send a cheque made payable to Compass Equestrian Ltd, or VISA/MASTERCARD details to Cadborough Farm, Oldberrow, Henley-in-Arden,Warwickshire, B95 5NX. Tel: 01564 795136

Name:

Address:

Signature:

VISA no:
Expiry date: